TO THE WOMAN I LOVE

Other books by Scott Matthews and Tamara Nikuradse
from Random House Value Publishing:

Dear Mom

Dear Dad

To the Man I Love
(by Tamara)

TO THE WOMAN I LOVE

Scott Matthews

GRAMERCY BOOKS
NEW YORK

This 2007 edition is published by Gramercy Books, an imprint of Random House Value Publishing, a division of Random House, Inc., New York.

Previously published as *To the Woman I Love, Thank You for Being Mine*
by Scott Matthews and Tamara Nikuradse

Gramercy is a registered trademark and the colophon is a trademark of Random House, Inc.

Random House
New York • Toronto • London • Sydney • Auckland
www.randomhouse.com

Interior book design by Christine Kell.

Printed and bound in Singapore.

A catalog record for this title is available from the Library of Congress.

ISBN: 978-0-517-22991-0

10 9 8 7 6 5 4 3 2 1

INTRODUCTION

In keeping with the spirit of the two previous books, *Dear Mom* and *Dear Dad*, I co-authored with my wife, Tamara Nikuradse, we wanted to thank one another for the love, support, understanding, and for all the many things that we have given to each other during our many years together. This book is inspired by those years.

I hope the following thank-yous spark special memories for you and inspire you to write your own thank-yous to the woman you love. Your words and expressions of love will make this collection even more meaningful. Feel free to cross out words and personalize the thank-yous or enter your special thank-yous on the blank page at the end of the book. If some of the thank-yous written in this book do not apply to your love, and you want them to, why not drop the hint by writing *(HINT... HINT...)* or *NOT!!!* after the thank-you in the book. Enjoy!

SCOTT

To the Woman I Love,
Thank you . . .

*T*hank you for being my love at first sight.

*T*hank you for not telling me to "get lost"
when I asked you for a date.

*T*hank you for a great first date from start to finish.

*T*hank you for returning my call after the first date.

*T*hank you for that first kiss, which will last a lifetime.

*T*hank you for making my dreams come true by
going out on a second date with me.

*T*hank you for giving your old beaus pink slips when a fortune-teller told you a handsome, intelligent, worldly, aristocratic gentleman with a great personality and rippling biceps would sweep you off your feet.

*T*hank you for letting me be that gentleman.

*T*hank you for promoting me from friend to boyfriend and letting me call you "babe" in private.

*T*hank you for showing up at my office door at lunchtime with a picnic basket.

*T*hank you for winning a huge stuffed animal for me at the amusement park.

*T*hank you for treating me to an espresso at a sidewalk café after a Saturday night movie.

*T*hank you for making goofy faces with me in a photo booth.

*T*hank you for riding with me on a merry-go-round.

*T*hank you for taking me on an elephant ride at
the "Greatest Show on Earth."

*T*hank you for overcoming your butterflies and singing "My Guy"
to me in front of a roomful of strangers at a karaoke bar.

*T*hank you for seeing a horror film with me and
grabbing my arm at the scary parts.

*T*hank you for not being a "fatal attraction."

*T*hank you for taking me on a horse-and-buggy ride.

*T*hank you for meeting me in the middle when we both started chewing
at different ends of the same licorice stick.

*T*hank you for taking me to my favorite Chinese restaurant
and insisting on paying the bill.

*T*hank you for knocking me off my feet when you said, "I love you."

*T*hank you for spraying your love letters with perfume
and stamping them with lipstick kisses.

Thank you for storing my love letters to you in a safe and secure place where no one will ever find them.

Thank you for tying cans to the back of my car and taping a "Just in Love!" sign on the trunk.

Thank you for sitting with me in the front seat of a roller coaster and screaming like a maniac with your arms in the air.

Thank you for being my not-so-secret admirer.

Thank you for playing the combination of our birthdays in the lottery in the hope of escaping to some tropical island in the South Pacific, far from the madding crowd, where we can sip margaritas while lounging on beach chaises.

Thank you for telling me that you've already won the jackpot because you have me, and the annuity pays out over a lifetime.

Thank you for e-mailing love poems to me that promise a wonderful life together.

*T*hank you for holding my hand during doubleheaders.

*T*hank you for not getting too jealous when there's a message on my
answering machine from an old girlfriend.

*T*hank you for telling me to go fly a kite—and then
flying one with me in the park.

*T*hank you for leaving behind Hershey's Kisses when you
couldn't be there to kiss me in person.

*T*hank you for not entering our relationship with
preconceived notions or a rule book.

*T*hank you for placing a newspaper ad declaring your love for me.

*T*hank you for calling me every night before you went to sleep just to say,
"I love you."

*T*hank you for holding me close during our moonlight strolls.

*T*hank you for practicing safe sex before you met me.

*T*hank you for waiting until I was ready to go all the way.

*T*hank you for making our "first time" together the most incredible
and unforgettable experience ever!

*T*hank you for waking up with a smile on your face instead of pretending
that the night before didn't happen and running out the door.

*T*hank you for respecting me in the morning.

*T*hank you for feeling comfortable enough with me to let me
see you without your makeup on.

*T*hank you for finally giving me a key to your place and my
very own corner to throw my clothes in.

*T*hank you for wanting me to meet my parents.

*T*hank you for impressing my family with your grace,
wit, charm, and intelligence.

*T*hank you for complimenting my parents without making it *too* obvious.

*T*hank you for sneaking into my bedroom for a little hanky-panky in the middle of the night when we stayed at my parents' house.

*T*hank you for not getting caught.

*T*hank you for warning me what to say and what not to say to your parents before our first meeting.

*T*hank you for warning me about your father's plan to interrogate me about my intentions.

*T*hank you for bringing me to a family reunion and not abandoning me with your talkative Uncle Herb.

*T*hank you for stopping at a busy playground and dreaming of a day when we have children who will make this world a brighter place.

*T*hank you for walking barefoot on a deserted beach with me during the off season.

*T*hank you for spending a rainy fall afternoon with me in an art museum.

*T*hank you for being my homecoming date and a good sport as you sat
on the cold, wet bleachers during the football game.

*T*hank you for dressing up with me as Romeo and Juliet on Halloween.

*T*hank you for rolling with me in a pile of leaves
and letting me be on top.

*T*hank you for picking a bushel of apples and
baking an apple pie with me.

*T*hank you for making hay with me on the back of
a wagon during a hayride.

*T*hank you for cooking a scrumptious Thanksgiving feast
with me for my relatives.

*T*hank you for calling my favorite radio station to have *our* song
dedicated to me during my morning drive.

*T*hank you for hiding love notes in my suit pocket, my wallet, and my car.

*T*hank you for sparing me the fun and adventure of baby
showers and cat shows.

*T*hank you for playing footsie with me under my parents' table
during dinner parties.

*T*hank you for setting the timer on the camera so
we'd have a picture of us.

*T*hank you for doodling hearts around our initials.

*T*hank you for wearing strapless dresses that accentuate your cleavage.

*T*hank you for giving me a "pettifore" by clipping my toenails.

*T*hank you for playing hooky from work with me and going to a matinee.

*T*hank you for feeding me chocolate covered strawberries in bed.

*T*hank you for watching "Frosty the Snowman," "The Grinch Who Stole
Christmas," "Rudolph the Red Nosed Reindeer," and "Santa Claus Is
Coming to Town" year after year after year.

Thank you for braving the Christmas crowds to shop with me
up to the last minute.

Thank you for making shopping for your gifts an easy expedition by
dropping discreet hints (like drawing big red circles around certain items
in catalogs and marking the circles with exclamation points).

Thank you for teaching me how to wrap gifts properly so they don't look
like something that goes out with the trash.

Thank you for kissing me whenever we stand under mistletoe.

Thank you for not baking fruitcakes for my relatives.

Thank you for putting up with my protests when I didn't want to go to
The Nutcracker for the second year in a row.

Thank you for not being a nutcracker.

Thank you for being my secret Santa and not stuffing
my stocking with coal.

*T*hank you for celebrating our very own Christmas before we visited our relatives.

*T*hank you for kissing me at midnight and making shared promises with me for our New Year together.

*T*hank you for not breaking too many of your New Year's resolutions by the second week in January.

*T*hank you for throwing the first snowball to start a snowball fight.

*T*hank you for building a snowman in the park and letting me decapitate it before the neighborhood kids got the pleasure.

*T*hank you for trying to hold me up when you taught me how to skate.

*T*hank you for pulling off my winter boots and rubbing the blood back into my frozen toes after a romp in the snow.

*T*hank you for making me hot cocoa with those little marshmallows on a cold winter's eve.

*T*hank you for chasing away my winter blues with your warm smiles.

*T*hank you for buying salty snacks and beer and throwing a Super Bowl party for the two of us so we could cheer on our team.

*T*hank you for sharing your erotic dreams that included me and keeping quiet about those other dreams that didn't include me.

*T*hank you for removing the lint from my belly button.

*T*hank you for blowing sloppy wet kisses on my belly.

*T*hank you for attending an RV show with me and dreaming about our retirement, when we can spend every day together driving along Route 66.

*T*hank you for watching NASCAR races with me.

*T*hank you for doing the little things that make me happy just because.

*T*hank you for not plastering your face with makeup.

*T*hank you for declaring a "Honey Appreciation Day" and honoring me all day.

*T*hank you for scrubbing my back in the shower with a loofah pad.

*T*hank you for explaining what a loofah is.

*T*hank you for saying "YES!" when I popped the big question and saving me from a life of bachelorhood.

*T*hank you for acting surprised even though you expected the ring all along despite my best intentions to fake you out.

*T*hank you for understanding that the size of the diamond on your engagement ring does not measure my love for you.

*T*hank you for crying tears of happiness when it finally dawned on you that you'd be marrying me.

*T*hank you for preparing a Valentine's Day dinner of oysters with green M&Ms for dessert.

*T*hank you for being in the direct path of my Cupid's arrow.

*T*hank you for not checking us into a cheesy motel with mirrors on the ceiling and a vibrating bed that takes quarters as a Valentine's Day surprise.

Thank you for being my genie and granting me three wishes.

Thank you for granting my first wish when
you said you would marry me.

Thank you for granting my second wish when you said you'd
spend the rest of your life with me.

Thank you for granting my third wish when you said you'd
be the mother of our children.

Thank you for holding my hand in public no matter how sweaty it got.

Thank you for taking massage classes and demonstrating the
ancient techniques on me.

Thank you for building a photo shrine of me in your office and
on your screensaver.

Thank you for celebrating the anniversary of our first kiss.

Thank you for always fooling me on April 1st, like the time you applied a
temporary tattoo above your butt that read "Daddy's Girl."

*T*hank you for helping (and making) me meet my deadlines every April 15th.

*T*hank you for exchanging "I" for "we."

*T*hank you for taking me for a ride on a bicycle built for two and pedaling most of the way uphill.

*T*hank you for going to a Little League ball game, even when we don't know any of the players, so that I can relive the memories of the ball going through my legs.

*T*hank you for leaving sexy messages on my voice mail and in my e-mail box.

*T*hank you for not humming "Another One Bites the Dust," as I mourn the loss of yet another hair to my brush.

*T*hank you for finding the best seats at the theater-in-the-park.

*T*hank you for being my very own Victoria's Secret model.

*T*hank you for putting a little more emphasis in your derriere when you walk away from me.

*T*hank you for being my pillow.

*T*hank you for not talking to your plants more than you talk to me.

*T*hank you for writing "I love you" in the steam on the bathroom mirror.

*T*hank you for being the sexiest woman alive.

*T*hank you for putting together photo scrapbooks so that we can revisit all of our great times.

*T*hank you for snuggling with me under a quilt when I'm not feeling well.

*T*hank you for writing a fan letter telling me why you're my biggest fan.

*T*hank you for sending a card to my mother on Mother's Day thanking her for creating me.

*T*hank you for pitching a tent in the backyard and camping out.

*T*hank you for renting a room at a spa and hot-tubbing with me.

*T*hank you for surprising me with plane tickets to
a secret destination known only to you.

*T*hank you for packing my swim trunks, kidnapping me, and
taking me to a water amusement park.

*T*hank you for skinny dipping with me on a secluded beach.

*T*hank you for lying with me in an open field of cool grass on a summer
night, wishing upon a shooting star, and discussing how we
were lovers in a prior life.

*T*hank you for writing "I love you" in the air with sparklers
on the Fourth of July.

*T*hank you for not getting too mad when I threw you in the pool or
put an ice cube down your back.

*T*hank you for building sand castles with me.

*T*hank you for kicking the surf with me during a long walk on the beach.

*T*hank you for protecting me from UV rays by rubbing SPF 45
sun screen all over me (including my scalp).

*T*hank you for relinquishing control of the barbecue to me,
"King Potentate of All Barbecues, Master of All Grills."

*T*hank you for wearing short shorts on hot days.

*T*hank you for using Nair (and not my razor) for short shorts.

*T*hank you for cleaning my razor after you shave.

*T*hank you for exploring mountain trails on long hikes.

*T*hank you for learning to say "I love you" in seven foreign languages.

*T*hank you for not emasculating me with pruning shears
when I gave you cause.

*T*hank you for creating love coupons to be redeemed
for chores or fun favors.

Thank you for not ruining my shirts with lipstick smudges on my collars.

Thank you for licking off my milk mustache.

Thank you for finding out-of-the-way jazz bars with good bands.

Thank you for finding the perfect perch for gazing at a sunset with me.

Thank you for intoxicating me with the elixir of your love.

Thank you for loving me more than you love your cat.

Thank you for understanding that when my dog growls at you it is just jealousy.

Thank you for growing to tolerate my dog even though he slobbers all over you as a sign of affection (kind of like me).

Thank you for letting my dog take up one half of the couch and me the other half.

Thank you for not making me explain why my dog chases his tail.

*T*hank you for not hitting my dog every time he sniffs your most
intimate of areas. (Bad dog.)

*T*hank you for not hurting my dog's feelings by calling him
a stupid mutt.

*T*hank you for watching with me old "Saturday Night Live" reruns from
the days of Belushi and Radner.

*T*hank you for taking me to movies on sneak preview nights and
buying a large bucket of popcorn to share.

*T*hank you for recording your thoughts of love and slipping the CD in
my car's CD player as an early morning pick-me-up.

*T*hank you for not expecting me to go on your I-Have-to-Lose-10-More-
Pounds-to-Fit-into-My-Wedding-Dress Diet with you.

*T*hank you for not making me eat rice cakes and carrot sticks when
I was in the mood for potato chips and ice cream.

*T*hank you for fixing up some of my friends with your girlfriends.

*T*hank you for not holding it against me for too long when your girlfriends said my friends were butt-heads with only one thing on their minds.

*T*hank you for vowing never to fix up our friends again.

*T*hank you for fulfilling my rock-and-roll teen fantasy many, many years later by taking me to Aerosmith and Rolling Stones concerts.

*T*hank you for browsing in bookstores with me.

*T*hank you for coloring your roots when they grow out.

*T*hank you for not canceling the wedding after the 1,293 fights over the smallest details, like having tails or no tails for the groomsmen, whether or not to seat my single aunt at the table with the most eligible bachelors, my mother's involvement . . .

*T*hank you for agreeing to register at my favorite sports store.

*T*hank you for paring down your invitation list from 512, even though it meant your third cousin was left off the list.

Thank you for not making me sign a prenuptial agreement.

Thank you for swearing to me that you didn't stuff dollar bills down the pants of some sweaty Chippendale's dancer during your bachelorette party.

Thank you for not grilling me or my buddies about my bachelor party.

Thank you for not losing your cool 24 hours before the ceremony when my mom told you that I was allergic to lilies of the valley, the flowers in your bouquet. *Ah . . . Ah . . . Choo!*

Thank you for not making your cat your maid of honor.

Thank you for being the most beautiful bride ever to walk down the aisle.

Thank you for not forgetting your lines . . . *I do.*

Thank you for vowing to love, honor, and cherish me.

Thank you for crying tears of joy during the ceremony.

Thank you for making an honest man out of me!

Thank you for throwing your bouquet in the direction of my aunt.

Thank you for not *mooshing* the wedding cake all over my face
during the cake-cutting ceremony.

Thank you for insisting that our guests throw birdseed instead of rice
so that the birds could celebrate too.

Thank you for making our wedding day the happiest day of my life.

Thank you for writing my share of the thank-you notes that
I promised to write three months ago.

Thank you for our spare-no-expense, run-up-the-debt, all-night-
romps-in-the-bed honeymoon.

Thank you for grinning from ear to ear when you close your eyes and
relive our honeymoon.

Thank you for trying to convince my parents that they're not losing a son,
they're gaining a daughter.

Thank you for calling my dad "Dad."

Thank you for finally acquiescing and not throwing away my aunt's
wedding gift—her hand-crafted, one-of-a-kind, ah . . . thing.
What is it again?

Thank you for pulling *the thing* out of the closet when my aunt
came to visit.

Thank you for allowing me to be part of the birth control decision.

Thank you for not wanting twelve children.

Thank you for nibbling on my ear and nuzzling me in all the right places
to get me in the mood.

Thank you for kissing me with long, deep, moist, passionate kisses, as if
you had all the time in the world.

Thank you for screaming and moaning when I got it right.

Thank you for always moaning *my* name during intimate moments.

Thank you for making me see stars and rockets' red glare.

Thank you for the nights that never end and convalescing with me the morning after.

Thank you for showing me how much you love me every second of every hour of every day.

Thank you for driving nowhere special just to see what's there.

Thank you for putting quarters in the jukebox and selecting my favorite songs.

Thank you for watching "60 Minutes" with me every Sunday night.

Thank you for never doing anything bad that would attract the attention of Ed Bradley.

Thank you for including me in your wishes when you blow out candles.

Thank you for not throwing away my disco eight-track tapes, Little League trophies, Cub Scouts uniform, tattered *MAD* magazines, beer can collection, thousands of old car parts . . .

Thank you for the hall pass to go out with the guys.

Thank you for reminding me how much you trust me before I went to a bachelor party or out on the town with the guys.

Thank you for not giving me the third degree when I got home.

Thank you for tickling me in all the right places.

Thank you for not plucking my chest hairs.

Thank you for not offering to mow my hairy back.

Thank you for not coming to bed or running to the store with curlers in your hair.

Thank you for running your fingers through my thinning hair and trying to convince me that it isn't thinning.

Thank you for not suggesting that I go to Hair Club for Men or spray-paint my scalp.

*T*hank you for not telling me that bald is sexy.

*T*hank you for not yakking on the phone to your girlfriends
all night long.

*T*hank you for kissing me behind the knees.

*T*hank you for making a surprise guest appearance in my shower.

*T*hank you for spicing up TV dinners with candles, red wine, and
Louisiana hot sauce.

*T*hank you for taking a picture of me with Mickey at Disneyland.

*T*hank you for trying to curb your "moodiness" around me.

*T*hank you for explaining how your plumbing . . . *er* . . . anatomy works.

*T*hank you for letting me eat all of the peanuts in the Cracker Jack box.

*T*hank you for not practicing reverse psychology on me.

Thank you for blowing kisses to me across a crowded room.

Thank you for using your frequent-flyer miles on me.

Thank you for inducting me into the Mile High Club.

Thank you for letting the devil make you do it every so often.

Thank you for not bragging to your girlfriends about
my performance in the sack.

Thank you for making me blush when you read out loud the steamy
passages from trashy romance novels.

Thank you for laughing at those stupid guys on the reality TV shows.

Thank you for bringing tears to my eyes when you say
you couldn't live without me.

Thank you for bringing home an armful of travel brochures so that we
can plan the perfect escape.

Thank you for helping me tuck my shirttails into my pants.

Thank you for not flirting with other men.

Thank you for firmly stating "I've gotta man" when other men
flirt with you.

Thank you for preparing tea and scones on a quiet Sunday afternoon for
you, and nachos and beer for me.

Thank you for playing rub-a-dub-dub in the tub with me.

Thank you for being my rubber ducky and squeaking when I squeeze you.

Thank you for starting a pillow fight and letting me win sometimes.

Thank you for lazing in bed with me on a Saturday morning and
watching the Coyote chase the Road Runner.

Thank you for helping me finally figure out what a Venus butterfly is.

Thank you for still having a crush on me after all these years.

*T*hank you for snuggling with me in bed as we read.

*T*hank you for boosting my confidence with your words of encouragement.

*T*hank you for cleaning your hair from the sink drain.

*T*hank you for cleaning *my* hair from the sink drain.

*T*hank you for sending me five postcards over five straight days with one word written on each: Very, Love, I, Much, You.

*T*hank you for being my personal image consultant.

*T*hank you for not comparing me to other guys that you know, including your father.

*T*hank you for buying me a new ice cream when my scoop fell to the ground.

*T*hank you for cherishing our love.

*T*hank you for not making me explain why I enjoy watching Moe smack Curly.

*T*hank you for not being a sore loser when I beat you at strip checkers.

*T*hank you for greeting me at the front door wearing a red teddy and a smile.

*T*hank you for letting me watch you undress.

*T*hank you for not accusing me of having only one thing on my mind!

*T*hank you for not listening to the tick-tock of your biological clock.

*T*hank you for eating the charred mystery dinner that I cooked for you while keeping a smile on your face no matter how awful it tasted.

*T*hank you for not letting a broken fingernail ruin your day.

*T*hank you for buying the pump dispenser after I kept forgetting to put the cap on the toothpaste.

*T*hank you for not making me feel inadequate around cucumbers.

*T*hank you for not lying to me.

*T*hank you for starring in my daydreams.

*T*hank you for keeping our secrets secret.

*T*hank you for not letting us become a divorce statistic.

*T*hank you for promising to meet me in the afterlife so that we can spend an eternity together—even if you come back as a cat and I come back as a dog.

*T*hank you for warming my side of the bed before I get in.

*T*hank you for telling me about your day and asking about mine.

*T*hank you for not disturbing me as I sit on my throne with my newspaper.

*T*hank you for replacing the empty roll of toilet paper and not leaving me stranded.

*T*hank you for showing me that bathrooms can smell pleasant
with potpourri.

*T*hank you for writing a list of 99 original reasons why I'm special and
taking it to a copy center to have it bound just in time for my birthday.

*T*hank you for doing new things to your hair even when I didn't notice.

*T*hank you for not running away with your friends Thelma and Louise.

*T*hank you for feeding me the best-tasting fiber you can find
to keep me regular.

*T*hank you for finding bargains at the outlets.

*T*hank you for not telling me "I told you so" when I deserve it.

*T*hank you for leaving my holey socks and underwear alone.

*T*hank you for screening your calls and always taking mine.

*T*hank you for creating a playlist of our favorite songs on my iPod.

$\mathcal{T}$hank you for asking for the directions when I pulled into a gas station.

$\mathcal{T}$hank you for not wearing so much perfume that it lingers over you like a storm cloud.

$\mathcal{T}$hank you for kissing me every morning when we wake up despite my morning breath.

$\mathcal{T}$hank you for writing sexy messages in my date book telling me where I had to be and when and what to wear and what you're going to do to me.

$\mathcal{T}$hank you for all of our tender moments.

$\mathcal{T}$hank you for every so often greeting me as I step from the shower with a towel warmed by the dryer.

$\mathcal{T}$hank you for picking up my pile of clothes that don't make it to the hamper.

$\mathcal{T}$hank you for telling me the dirty jokes you hear at the office.

$\mathcal{T}$hank you for letting me use your moisturizer to soothe my razor burn.

*T*hank you for not being an authority on every subject. That's my job!

*T*hank you for not holding it against me that I don't have buns of steel.

*T*hank you for not bashing my "species" too hard.

*T*hank you for curling up on the sofa with me to watch old Clint Eastwood movies.

*T*hank you for running errands for me like picking up my shirts, returning my DVDs, shopping for my mom's birthday gifts . . .

*T*hank you for telling me that I'm the sexiest man alive despite my love handles.

*T*hank you for using your hair spray sparingly so that I can light a match in your presence.

*T*hank you for being a great Dr. Mom by kissing my boo-boos.

*T*hank you for watching out for my best interest.

*T*hank you for not throwing breakable objects (or any objects) at me.

*T*hank you for calling my cell phone, asking for my credit card number, and playing 1-900 with me.

*T*hank you for pulling most of the weight around the house (with me being that weight).

*T*hank you for not making me carry your purse in public.

*T*hank you for completing my thoughts and . . .

*T*hank you for not reminding me about my exercise equipment that is crammed in the back of the closet.

*T*hank you for keeping track of impending special dates like anniversaries and birthdays so that I don't forget.

*T*hank you for playing sex kitten every once in a while. *Meow* . . .

*T*hank you for saying how much you love the gifts that I picked out by myself—even the outfits that you wouldn't be caught dead in.

*T*hank you for not trying on every dress in the store before deciding which one to buy.

*T*hank you for not using the shower rod as a clothesline for your panty hose and lingerie.

*T*hank you for buying me flowers from street vendors, even though they're really for you.

*T*hank you for not Googling old flames.

*T*hank you for listening to me no matter how hard it gets at times.

*T*hank you for not wearing high heels that make you tower over me.

*T*hank you for wearing red pumps on special occasions.

*T*hank you for living up to your promise when you say, "Honest, you can tell me, I won't get upset."

*T*hank you for letting me play in the sports stores while you shop in the rest of the mall.

Thank you for not having your old boyfriend's name tattooed on your butt.

Thank you for redefining beauty and chic in all that you do.

Thank you for not spending all of Saturday at the beauty salon.

Thank you for not making me come out of hiding when you throw a baby shower for your friend in our living room.

Thank you for not coming out of hiding when I have the boys over to play poker, so we can smoke cigars and cuss and tell dirty jokes and drink beer . . .

Thank you for cheering me on at my softball games.

Thank you for making my favorite appetizer, Cheez Whiz spread on crackers, before my favorite dinner, hot wings and beer.

Thank you for letting the phone ring when we're rolling between red silk sheets.

*T*hank you for forbidden pleasures like a *ménage a trois* with you, me, and Mr. Bubble.

*T*hank you for not criticizing me in public.

*T*hank you for reassuring me when I'm in doubt.

*T*hank you for being civil to my frat brothers when they visited us for a three-day weekend.

*T*hank you for beating the national average for making love per week.

*T*hank you for fighting fair and not hitting below the belt.

*T*hank you for returning home to me a little calmer after storming out in anger.

*T*hank you for not recycling lame excuses like "It was on sale" or "I have a headache."

*T*hank you for being my steady Saturday night date until death do us part.

Thank you for being a tourist with me and exploring new cities by foot.

Thank you for leaving your Blackberry, cell phone, and laptop home when we go on vacations.

Thank you for not saying "you don't understand me" *too* often.

Thank you for making a roast with all the trimmings as a surprise when you came home from work early.

Thank you for being my dessert.

Thank you for shoving me in the right direction when I needed it most.

Thank you for reading *How to Make Love to a Man* and practicing on me.

Thank you for bowling with me and not laughing at my gutter balls.

Thank you for giving me the benefit of the doubt when you didn't know my Scrabble game words.

Thank you for waiting in a long line with me at the movie theater for a sci-fi movie that you didn't want to see.

Thank you for our afternoon delights.

Thank you for not calling me names that hurt.

Thank you for not letting your cold feet touch my warm body when you jump into bed.

Thank you for e-mailing cartoons and pictures for me to enjoy.

Thank you for being my security blanket.

Thank you for not taking away my other security blanket— the remote control.

Thank you for living with my "little" idiosyncrasies, like my urge to zap 62 TV channels in 22 seconds flat.

Thank you for teaching me how to count calories and fat grams.

Thank you for letting your imagination run wild when we make love.

Thank you for brushing the white specks and lint balls from my suit before I leave for work.

Thank you for not letting your daily horoscope influence your moods.

Thank you for replying "Now there's more for me to love" when I complain about the ten extra pounds I've gained over the years.

Thank you for leaving purple and red hickeys on places that I can cover up for work the next day.

Thank you for stopping me from worrying too much.

Thank you for offering me a breath mint when I needed one.

Thank you for not draping your arm around me in public like a "No Trespassing" sign.

Thank you for taking me away for some R&R and TLC at a little B&B.

Thank you for not playing tit for tat with me.

Thank you for not ordering anchovies on the pizza because you'll taste fishy.

*T*hank you for sharing everything with me, even the flu.

*T*hank you for not reading *Playgirl* to see how I stack up.

*T*hank you for finding my contact lens when
I thought it dropped down the drain.

*T*hank you for getting me out of that speeding ticket when you convinced
the police officer that you were pregnant and you had to pee *NOW!!!*

*T*hank you for encouraging me to wear boxer shorts around the house.

*T*hank you for not requesting that I shave on weekends.

*T*hank you for growing to love my parents and thinking of them as
your good friends.

*T*hank you for going to my reunion and not remarking about the effects
of gravity on my former girlfriends.

*T*hank you for wanting to live with me until 100 so that Willard Scott
will announce our birthdays.

*T*hank you for telling me when I'm wearing two different colored socks.

*T*hank you for suggesting a test run of the *Kama Sutra.*

*T*hank you for giving to charities that protect baby seals.

*T*hank you for always striving to do your best.

*T*hank you for not dressing like Cher at an Oscar night or Britney in a music video.

*T*hank you for letting me drive your car—all the time!

*T*hank you for not being a backseat driver.

*T*hank you for replying, "Infinity divided by one over infinity all to the infinite power," when I ask you, "How much do you love me?"

*T*hank you for introducing me to the incredibly smooth voice of Nat King Cole.

*T*hank you for letting me have the window seat on the plane.

Thank you for taking me to the aquarium and pointing out the fish that look and pucker like me.

Thank you for teaching me to care about things that are important to you.

Thank you for not applying your makeup while you're driving.

Thank you for playing couch potato with me in front of the TV on a Friday night after a tough week.

Thank you for never telling me the honeymoon's over.

Thank you for letting me cry on your shoulders.

Thank you for not making me buy your tampons in a crowded store.

Thank you for finding the best gifts for my parents.

Thank you for only eating garlic and onions when we both do.

Thank you for not getting *too* jealous when I speak with another woman.

*T*hank you for massaging my aching muscles after a workout on the tennis court.

*T*hank you for teaching me patience.

*T*hank you for not kicking me out of bed for eating crackers.

*T*hank you for sharing with me the kind of love that makes other people envious.

*T*hank you for insisting that you wouldn't sleep with George Clooney for a million bucks.

*T*hank you for putting romance back in my life.

*T*hank you for always calling me when you are going to be late.

*T*hank you for framing photos of us and placing them around the house so that I can always look at you.

*T*hank you for forgiving me when I have hurt your feelings.

*T*hank you for explaining why whites come out pink when washed with new reds.

*T*hank you for finding my socks that the washing machine ate.

*T*hank you for taking my clothes out of my bureau and refolding them for me.

*T*hank you for picking up where my mom left off.

*T*hank you for not leering at other guys in my presence—especially those young hunks on *American Idol* or other Fox TV shows.

*T*hank you for not tickling me when you play with my love handles.

*T*hank you for giving me that special medicine called "love" that no doctor could prescribe and no pharmacist could bottle and label.

*T*hank you for sharing *The Joy of Sex* with me!

*T*hank you for not answering "I dunno, what do you want to do?" every time I ask, "What do you wanna do?"

*T*hank you for not singing "Rise and Shine!" in my ear at
6 A.M. on our days off.

*T*hank you for not being *too* competitive with me.

*T*hank you for disclosing your hidden agendas.

*T*hank you for being there at the end of "one of those days" and
reminding me of all the good things we have, like our health,
our family, our love, each other.

*T*hank you for being a trouper and going to the store to buy beer.

*T*hank you for juggling all that you do.

*T*hank you for having realistic expectations of me.

*T*hank you for keeping me young.

*T*hank you for not threatening me with "... or else!"

*T*hank you for your woman's intuition.

*T*hank you for keeping the lights on so that we can look into each other's
eyes when we make love.

*T*hank you for indulging the boy in me with uninterrupted
video game playtime.

*T*hank you for taking the blame to help me save face.

*T*hank you for tossing a Frisbee with me and my dog.

*T*hank you for swinging with me—on a schoolyard swing set, that is!

*T*hank you for spending your pay raises on me.

*T*hank you for seducing me in the back of a limo.

*T*hank you for not acting like the women on those reality TV shows.

*T*hank you for not disclosing the office gossip that I share with you and
getting me in trouble when you meet my friends from work.

*T*hank you for not whining like Daddy's little girl and pouting
when you don't get your way.

*T*hank you for letting me blast the air conditioning to get the room temperature down to 60 degrees.

*T*hank you for my special nicknames.

*T*hank you for not calling me by my special nicknames in public.

*T*hank you for not scheduling appointments for us to make love.

*T*hank you for investing in our relationship by doing those quizzes in the women's magazines.

*T*hank you for not believing the answers to those quizzes that say you need to find a new lover.

*T*hank you for not holding a grudge against me for the rest of my life and plotting ways to get even with me.

*T*hank you for helping me with crossword puzzles.

*T*hank you for letting me have the last word every once in a while.

*T*hank you for reminding me to slow down when you see that I get overwhelmed with stress.

*T*hank you for reading my mind.

*T*hank you for never going to bed mad at me or banishing me to the couch.

*T*hank you for checking my body for ticks after romps in the woods.

*T*hank you for not expecting me to be perfect.

*T*hank you for my Odor-Eaters.

*T*hank you for patting me on the back for a job well done.

*T*hank you for wearing fish-net stockings and stiletto heels—just once.

*T*hank you for letting me use your toothbrush.

*T*hank you for adding to my collection of power tools.

Thank you for leaving my power tools alone.

Thank you for not patronizing me.

Thank you for not using my mom as your role model.

Thank you for buying me new socks to replace the old ones that keep falling down around my ankles.

Thanks you for saving a little bit of room in the bedroom closet for me.

Thank you for letting me pick from your dinner plate.

Thank you for telling me when I've had too much to drink.

Thank you for stopping along the highway so that I can pee in the bushes.

Thank you for not using all the hot water during your showers or flushing the toilet when I'm in the shower.

Thank you for understanding that I'm unable to be romantic every day— but I'm trying!!!

*T*hank you for not breaking my heart.

*T*hank you for believing me when I say, "I'm sorry."

*T*hank you for always being in my corner and urging me on
between the rounds.

*T*hank you for dazzling me.

*T*hank you for sharing your dreams with me.

*T*hank you for exploring new worlds with me.

*T*hank you for being my hero.

*T*hank you for making me laugh.

*T*hank you for vowing to love me until the end of time.

*T*hank you for your faith in me.

*T*hank you for being the perfect mate in this life, as well as
in prior and future lives.

*T*hank you for making me your number-one priority.

*T*hank you for not raining on my parades.

*T*hank you for sharing the good, the bad, and even the ugly with me.

*T*hank you for filling my emotional needs.

*T*hank you for being my *bestest* friend in the whole wide world.

*T*hank you for making a commitment to us.

*T*hank you for taking care of me.

*T*hank you for the daily dose of joy and laughter that you bring into my life.

*T*hank you for your kindness and compassion.

*T*hank you for telling me that "I'd like a son just like you."

*T*hank you for being my number-one fan.

Thank you for smiling—a lot.

Thank you for accepting me for who I am.

Thank you for waiting all of your life for me.

Thank you for starting our own traditions.

Thank you for telling me that time began when you met me.

Thank you for being you.

Thank you for being mine—always and forever.

Special Thank-Yous Just for the Woman I Love

$\mathcal{T}$hank you _____

$\mathcal{T}$hank you _____

$\mathcal{T}$hank you _____

$\mathcal{T}$hank you _____

$\mathcal{T}$hank you _____

$\mathcal{T}$hank you _____

$\mathcal{T}$hank you _____

$\mathcal{T}$hank you _____

$\mathcal{T}$hank you _____

ABOUT THE AUTHOR

Scott Matthews is married to Tamara Nikuradse. He has co-authored fourteen books.

Don't Forget the Man You Love!

*T*hank you for asking me for a date instead of hitting me over the head with your club and dragging me by my hair back to your cave.

*T*hank you for not considering dinner on our first date as foreplay.

*T*hank you for not expecting a reward like a barking seal every time you perform a chore.

*T*hank you for not zapping the channels with the remote (*hint . . . hint . . .*).

*T*hank you for sending a card to my mother on Mother's Day thanking her for creating me.

ASK FOR *TO THE MAN I LOVE* AT YOUR FAVORITE BOOKSELLER.